Alfred's
INSTRUMENTAL
PLAY-ALONG

Favorite HYMNS
INSTRUMENTAL SOLOS

Arranged by Bill Galliford, Ethan Neuburg and Tod Edmondson

Alfred Cares. Contents printed on recycled paper.

© 2010 Alfred Music Publishing Co., Inc.
All Rights Reserved. Printed in USA.

Alfred

ISBN-10: 0-7390-7180-7
ISBN-13: 978-0-7390-7180-9

Photograph sourtesy of Barry Erra

MW00379318

—Contents—

AMAZING GRACE

TRADITIONAL AMERICAN MELODY

4

ALL CREATURES OF OUR GOD AND KING

Track 4: Demo
Track 5: Play Along

By St. FRANCIS of ASSISI and
GEISTLICHE KIRCHENGESANGE, COLOGNE

36124

HOLY, HOLY, HOLY! LORD GOD ALMIGHTY

Track 6: Demo
Track 7: Play Along

By JOHN B. DYKES
and REGINAL HEBER

Moderately slow, flowing ♩ = 88

JOYFUL, JOYFUL, WE ADORE THEE

Track 8: Demo
Track 9: Play Along

By HENRY VAN DYKE
and LUDWIG VAN BEETHOVEN

36124

A MIGHTY FORTRESS IS OUR GOD

Track 10: Demo
Track 11: Play Along

By MARTIN LUTHER

36124

Track 12: Demo
Track 13: Play Along

BE THOU MY VISION

Moderately ♩ = 104

TRADITIONAL IRISH HYMN

IT IS WELL WITH MY SOUL

By HORATIO G. SPAFFORD
and PHILIP P. BLISS

Track 14: Demo
Track 15: Play Along

Moderate gospel feel ♩ = 104

36124

GREAT IS THY FAITHFULNESS

Track 16: Demo
Track 17: Play Along

Music by
WILLIAM M. RUNYAN

Great Is Thy Faithfulness - 2 - 1
36124

HIS EYE IS ON THE SPARROW

Track 18: Demo
Track 19: Play Along

By CIVILLA D. MARTIN
and CHARLES H. GABRIEL

Gently, with expression (♩ = 108)

Verse:

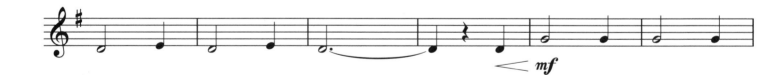

His Eye Is on the Sparrow - 2 - 1
36124

HOW GREAT THOU ART

Track 20: Demo
Track 21: Play Along

Words and Music by
STUART K. HINE

O THE DEEP, DEEP LOVE OF JESUS

Track 22: Demo
Track 23: Play Along

By SAMUEL TREVOR FRANCIS
and THOMAS J. WILLIAMS

O the Deep, Deep Love of Jesus - 2 - 1
36124

O the Deep, Deep Love of Jesus - 2 - 2
36124

'TIS SO SWEET TO TRUST IN JESUS

Track 24: Demo
Track 25: Play Along

Moderate folk style (♩ = 82)

By LOUISA M. R. STEAD
and WILLIAM J. KIRKPATRICK

PARTS OF THE HORN AND FINGERING CHART

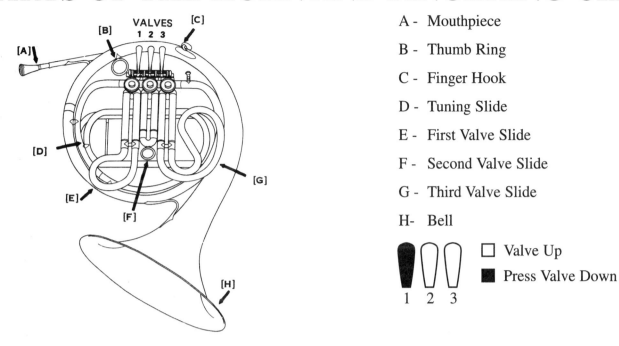

VALVES
1 2 3

[A]
[B] [C]
[D]
[E] [F]
[G]
[H]

A - Mouthpiece

B - Thumb Ring

C - Finger Hook

D - Tuning Slide

E - First Valve Slide

F - Second Valve Slide

G - Third Valve Slide

H- Bell

☐ Valve Up

■ Press Valve Down

1 2 3

F Horns use the top fingerings. B♭ Horns use the bottom fingerings. F/B♭ Double Horns use the top fingerings without the thumb, or the bottom fingerings with the thumb. A good rule is to play notes from the second line G down on the F Horn, and from the second line G♯ up on the B♭ Horn.

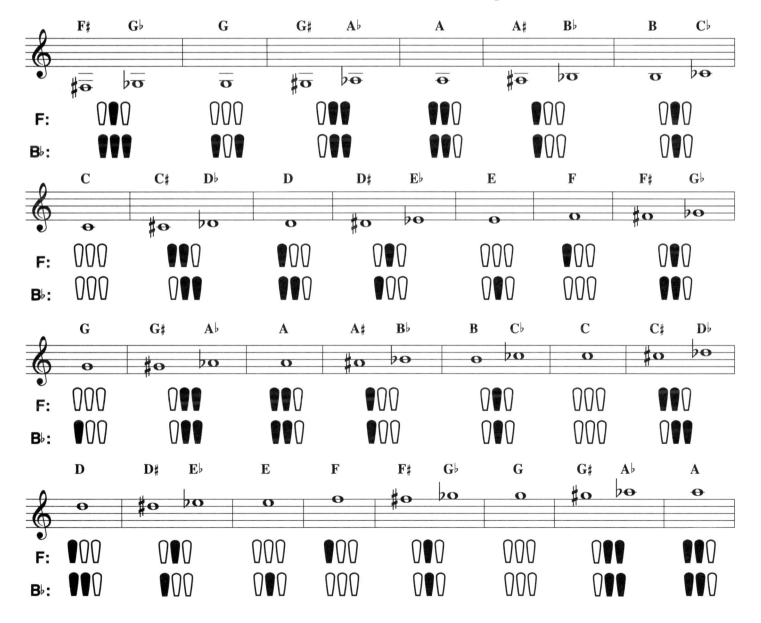